POP BUCHANAN

Inves AI Crypto

The Investor's Guide to Artificial Intelligence, Machine Learning, Quantum Computing, and the Top Cryptocurrency Blockchains from Bitcoin to Solana to Bittensor and DePIN Networks

INVEST AI CRYPTO: FINANCIAL DISCLAIMER

Important Notice: The information contained in Invest AI Crypto is presented for educational and entertainment purposes only. Nothing in this book should be interpreted as financial, investment, tax, or legal advice. It is not a solicitation, recommendation, or endorsement to buy, sell, or hold any cryptocurrency, token, security, or financial instrument.

All examples, companies, and digital assets discussed in this publication are provided to illustrate ideas and trends. Readers must conduct their own independent research and should consult licensed financial advisors or registered investment professionals before making any financial decisions.

Cryptocurrency and digital asset markets are highly volatile and speculative. Prices can change dramatically in short periods of time, and investors may lose some or all of their capital. Past performance is never a guarantee of future results. Pop Buchanan, Sober Is Dope Publishing, and all related entities make no guarantees or warranties of any kind regarding financial outcomes, market behavior, or investment performance.

Any statements about future trends, blockchain growth, artificial intelligence, or emerging technologies are based on available data and informed observation. These subjects evolve quickly and involve many uncertainties. Regulation, innovation, or external events may alter or invalidate certain projections. Readers must take full responsibility for their investment choices and financial risk.

By reading Invest AI Crypto, you acknowledge that you are solely responsible for your financial actions. You agree that neither the author nor the publisher shall be held liable for any loss, damages, or claims that may arise from the use or interpretation of this material.

This book exists to educate and to inspire curiosity about technology and innovation. It is not written to influence or direct individual investment activity.

First edition

This book was professionally typeset on Reedsy.
Find out more at reedsy.com

Dedication

To everyone who missed Bitcoin,
this book is for you.

May it open your eyes to the next wave of innovation,
and remind you that opportunity never truly disappears.
It only changes form.

The next big thing is already taking shape.
All you need is the courage to see it,
and the wisdom to act when it arrives.

~ Pop Buchanan

Contents

1

The Blockchain Age of Intelligence

When I started writing the Invest AI series, I wanted to help people see the future before it became the present. Invest AI was born from curiosity. Invest AI Quantum opened the door to quantum computing. Invest AI Robotics explored the machines that move and think. Now, it is time to look at the final link in the chain: the blockchain.

Every new era in technology starts with a simple idea that spreads until the world cannot live without it. The internet gave us information. Artificial intelligence gave us understanding. Blockchain gives us trust. When we connect all three, we get something powerful: a world where machines can think, act, and prove what they did without human permission. That is the machine economy, and it is already here.

I have spent years watching this world unfold from the inside. I have seen small teams with big dreams create tools that challenge entire industries. I have seen how cryptocurrency became more than money. It became energy. It became data. It became a new way to organize human and machine effort.

This book is not about gambling on coins or chasing trends. It is about understanding the structure that supports artificial intelligence, robotics, and the new generation of decentralized networks. I want every reader, whether a student, engineer, or investor, to see how this next evolution connects. Because when you understand the connections, you see opportunities that most people miss.

In Invest AI: Crypto, I will show how the blockchain, artificial intelligence, and machine learning are merging into one system of intelligence. We will explore how DePINs, quantum computing, and new crypto projects form the foundation of the next global economy. And we will talk about Bitcoin, Solana, Ethereum, and the dozens of other blockchains that are building the future right now.

This is not science fiction. It is happening as you read this sentence. The future of AI runs on chips, data, and trust. Blockchain gives that trust a permanent home. Together, they form the nervous system of a new world.

So take a deep breath, open your mind, and get ready to see how the intelligence of machines is finding its soul in the blockchain.

2

When AI Met Crypto

I remember the first time I heard someone say, "AI is the brain, and blockchain is the memory." It sounded poetic, but it was also true. Artificial intelligence creates understanding. Blockchain records that understanding forever. When you combine them, you get a digital mind that can think, act, and verify its own actions.

The story of how AI met crypto starts with Bitcoin. In 2008, Satoshi Nakamoto released a short white paper that changed history. He described a network that allowed strangers to agree on the same truth without a middleman (Nakamoto, 2008). That single idea; shared truth, became the foundation for everything that came after.

For years, blockchain stayed focused on money. People traded coins and argued about price. But hidden inside Bitcoin's design was something much bigger. It was a system that allowed digital agents to coordinate without trust. That meant one day, artificial intelligence could use it too.

Fast forward to today. AI has become the world's most powerful engine for learning. It trains on data, improves itself, and makes predictions that fuel entire industries. But AI has a problem: it needs reliable data and clear ownership. Models cannot learn from data they do not trust or own. That is where blockchain steps in.

Blockchains keep a permanent record of every action, file, or transaction. Each block links to the next, forming a digital ledger that cannot be easily changed. It is like giving AI a notebook it can never lose or erase. Every time an AI model uses data, a blockchain can record it. Every time it trains or improves, the change can be verified. This builds accountability into intelligence.

Projects like **Bittensor, SingularityNET, and Ocean Protocol** are showing what this future looks like. They let people share computing power, data, and algorithms through decentralized markets. Instead of giant corporations controlling AI models, anyone can contribute and earn from their participation (Bittensor Foundation, 2025; SingularityNET, 2024; Ocean Protocol, 2024). It is the start of an open AI economy.

Think about that for a moment. AI models that trade resources with each other. Machines that pay for GPU power, data storage, or even robot labor. Every one of those transactions needs a record and a currency. Blockchain provides both. It is the backbone of digital cooperation.

Another way AI and blockchain connect is through security. AI systems depend on data integrity. If someone manipulates data, it can ruin the model's output. With blockchain, that data becomes tamper-proof. Hospitals can store patient data safely. Supply chains can track materials from factory to shelf. Autonomous vehicles can log every movement without risk of fraud.

The relationship also works in reverse. AI makes blockchain smarter. Machine learning helps identify fraud, predict network congestion, and optimize smart contract execution. Together, they create self-improving systems that manage themselves with little human input.

As I researched for this book, I realized something simple but profound: AI and crypto are not separate revolutions. They are two halves of one story. The same people building AI systems are now building decentralized networks to run them. The same GPUs that train ChatGPT models are used to secure blockchain consensus. The same investors funding robotics are now looking at tokenized infrastructure.

When I say we are entering the machine economy, I mean it literally. Every machine, from your car to your coffee maker, will soon have a wallet. It will pay for power, data, and updates automatically. It will communicate with other machines, and the blockchain will keep everyone honest.

This is the dawn of digital autonomy. Humans will still design and supervise, but machines will handle the micro-transactions that keep the world running. Imagine solar panels selling energy to the grid, delivery drones paying for airspace, or personal AIs renting extra storage when needed. That is not far away.

Some people call this the Internet of Value. I call it the Internet of Intelligence. The next economy is not just digital; it is alive with decision-making systems that can act independently and fairly.

When AI met crypto, the world gained a new operating system. It is transparent, decentralized, and borderless. It rewards contribution instead of control. It is the start of a future where value moves at the speed of thought.

And we are just getting started.

3

The Supply Chain of Intelligence

To understand how to invest in the future, you have to understand where intelligence begins. It does not start in the cloud or inside an app. It starts with metal, sand, and math. Every piece of artificial intelligence runs on a chain of physical parts and invisible code that stretches across the planet. That chain is the new supply line of human progress.

When I talk about the supply chain of intelligence, I am talking about the journey from atoms to algorithms. It begins with the chips that process information. The chip is the brain cell of the machine age. Companies like NVIDIA, AMD, and Intel make the processors that power robots, blockchains, and AI models (McKinsey & Company, 2024). These chips are not just parts. They are factories of thought.

Every time a neural network trains, every time a blockchain validates a transaction, those tiny silicon squares burn electricity and turn it into intelligence. The more powerful the chip, the faster the world learns. That is why semiconductor stocks have become the new oil. They power both data and trust.

But chips alone cannot make a machine intelligent. They need eyes and ears. That is where sensors come in. Cameras, LiDAR, and radar systems give robots and autonomous cars the ability to see. Microphones and environmental sensors let them hear and feel. Each sensor feeds data into AI models, and that data becomes the raw material for learning.

The next stop in the chain is connectivity. Every robot, car, and AI model has to communicate. This is where the blockchain joins the picture. Networks like Solana, Polygon, and Avalanche make it possible for machines to record, verify, and send information without relying on one central system (CoinDesk Research, 2025). It is digital conversation that never loses its memory.

When I first studied this ecosystem, I realized something powerful. Every company in this chain is a business by itself, but together they form a living system. The GPU makers build the compute. The sensor companies supply perception. The blockchain networks create the trust layer. The data platforms feed the brain. The energy companies keep it all running.

Investing in robotics or crypto is really about investing in this entire web. You are not just buying coins or chips. You are buying a piece of the world's digital nervous system.

One example is Render Network. Render connects artists and developers to unused GPU power. People rent their graphics cards to others through blockchain contracts, earning tokens while helping create visual effects, games, and AI art. Another example is Akash Network, which provides decentralized cloud computing for AI developers. These projects take something we once centralized—computing—and spread it across millions of users (Render Network Foundation, 2025; Akash Network, 2025).

This model creates what I call the "energy of intelligence." Machines need power, computation, and data to stay alive. When people share those resources through decentralized markets, value becomes global. It does not matter where you live or what language you speak. If you have power to share, the network rewards you. That is the foundation of the machine economy.

Semiconductors also connect directly to crypto mining. Bitcoin miners use chips to solve puzzles and secure the blockchain. The process looks wasteful to some, but it built an industry that forced innovation in chip design. The same efficiency that helped Bitcoin now fuels AI hardware. NVIDIA's chips train large language models by doing what Bitcoin miners did first; turning math into consensus.

When you follow this thread, you see a single story. From the silicon mines of Taiwan and Arizona to the data centers of Iceland and Singapore, the supply chain of intelligence is one giant loop. Chips make data. Data trains AI. AI runs on blockchains. Blockchains record AI behavior. It is a circle of learning and proof.

In the next decade, this loop will only tighten. The rise of Decentralized Physical Infrastructure Networks, DePINs, will bring this system closer to the real world. Solar farms, drones, and electric vehicles will all connect through tokens and smart contracts. Machines will buy and sell compute power, rent storage, and share data directly. Humans will set the rules, but the machines will handle the flow.

The message is simple. If you want to see where value is moving, follow the flow of intelligence. Follow the chips, the code, and the chain that links them. This is not speculation. It is the new infrastructure of life.

We are no longer just connecting people to the internet. We are connecting machines to each other, creating an economy that runs on thought. And the deeper we go, the more we realize that intelligence itself has become the ultimate resource.

4

Decentralized Physical Infrastructure Networks (DePINs)

When I first heard the term "DePIN," it sounded like another crypto buzzword. Then I looked deeper and realized it could be one of the most important inventions of our time. Decentralized Physical Infrastructure Networks connect the physical world to the blockchain. They let real people and real machines earn tokens for providing real-world services.

This means you can build a digital network that runs on physical devices; everything from Wi-Fi routers to delivery drones. Every person who connects a device becomes part of the system and gets rewarded for helping it grow. It is the first time in history that physical infrastructure has been crowdsourced and owned by the people who power it.

To understand DePINs, picture how the internet began. In the early days, only big companies could build data centers. Now anyone can help power decentralized networks by sharing hardware, bandwidth, or energy. The blockchain keeps the system fair, and tokens keep everyone motivated to contribute.

One of the best examples is Helium. Helium started as a small project that wanted to build a decentralized wireless network. Instead of asking a giant telecom company to build towers, Helium invited regular people to plug in small hotspots at home. Each hotspot shared wireless coverage and earned Helium tokens (HNT) for helping others connect (Helium Foundation, 2024). Within two years, Helium had more than one million active hotspots across the world.

Another example is Filecoin. Filecoin pays people to share unused hard-drive space. When you store a file on the Filecoin network, it is saved across many computers, not just one data center (Protocol Labs, 2024). This creates a safer, more open internet. It is like Airbnb for data storage.

Then there is IoTeX, which connects Internet of Things (IoT) devices through blockchain. It lets smart devices like sensors, cameras, and even vehicles exchange verified data and payments directly with each other (IoTeX Foundation, 2025). Imagine a world where a self-driving car pays a smart traffic light to change at the right moment. That is where we are heading.

Together, these projects show what makes DePIN special: it connects the virtual world of crypto with the real world of machines and humans. You can touch the hardware, feel the energy, and watch the tokens move.

The economic model behind DePINs is simple. Each device contributes something valuable; storage, computing power, network coverage, or data. The blockchain measures that contribution and rewards the provider with tokens. This system cuts out middlemen and replaces traditional ownership with community participation.

During my research, I noticed a new wave of DePIN projects growing fast. Render Network pays users to share unused GPU power for AI and visual effects. Akash Network does the same for cloud computing. Hivemapper rewards drivers for mapping roads with dash cameras. WeatherXM pays users to run weather stations that feed real-time climate data into a global model

(Render Network Foundation, 2025; Akash Network, 2025; Hivemapper, 2024; WeatherXM, 2025).

Each of these projects represents a small piece of the same dream: to build a global infrastructure owned by people, powered by machines, and balanced by code. This is the backbone of the machine economy.

DePINs are not only about profit. They change how communities can organize. In the old world, building infrastructure took billions of dollars and government approval. Now, a group of neighbors can deploy a small wireless network, share solar energy, or track air quality together. The token model turns participation into a form of ownership.

That is why DePINs are attracting attention from AI developers and robotics companies. Robots and AI systems need networks they can trust, and DePINs offer both coverage and accountability. A robot that depends on a DePIN for navigation or data storage can operate anywhere without relying on one corporation's servers.

Think about how powerful that becomes when combined with AI. A fleet of delivery drones could deliver packages, share maps, and get paid instantly through blockchain. A smart city could run on decentralized power grids that trade energy automatically. Every action, from charging a robot to sending a signal, would be recorded and verified.

The more I studied it, the more I realized this was the bridge between the physical and digital worlds. DePINs are not science fiction. They are the first real example of machines earning income. And they are already alive today, humming quietly in homes, vehicles, and devices across the globe.

The next step is scale. As AI and robotics expand, DePINs will grow into the invisible infrastructure that keeps the world running. They will connect solar farms, factories, autonomous cars, and home networks into one web of shared intelligence. Humans will still lead, but our machines will handle the flow of data, power, and payment with perfect precision.

This is what the new industrial revolution looks like. It is powered by code, sustained by community, and guided by intelligence.

In the next chapter, we will explore the Top 50 Blockchains that power this world; what they do, why they matter, and how each plays a role in the intelligence economy.

5

The Top Blockchains and Why They Matter

When people hear the word "blockchain," they often think of Bitcoin and nothing else. They imagine a single digital coin. But the blockchain world is not one idea. It is a universe of innovation, full of networks that power everything from finance to artificial intelligence. Each chain has its own mission, its own rules, and its own vision for the future.

Writing this book reminded me how alive this world really is. It is not a game of traders and charts. It is the next layer of the internet, a living system that connects data, people, and machines. Each blockchain we explore in this chapter adds one piece to the new machine economy.

Let's begin with the foundations.

Bitcoin – The Digital Root of Trust

Bitcoin is the original blockchain. It started in 2008 when Satoshi Nakamoto released a nine-page paper that changed the world (Nakamoto, 2008). Bitcoin created the first form of digital money that required no bank and no government. It runs on math, not authority.

Bitcoin is the most secure and time-tested blockchain on Earth. Its strength is honesty. Every ten minutes, computers all around the world confirm the same truth. That trust makes Bitcoin the base layer of value in the digital economy.

Even in the age of artificial intelligence, Bitcoin matters. Machines need a currency they can trust, and Bitcoin offers that foundation. It is slow on purpose because speed is not its goal. Its goal is permanence.

Ethereum – The Operating System of Smart Contracts

Ethereum took Bitcoin's core idea and made it programmable. Instead of storing only money, Ethereum can store logic. This means developers can create smart contracts, which are self-running pieces of code that execute agreements automatically (Buterin, 2015).

Smart contracts make it possible for AI agents, DePINs, and robotics systems to operate independently. They let machines pay each other, rent data, or trigger tasks. Ethereum also paved the way for the explosion of DeFi, NFTs, and DAOs—decentralized autonomous organizations that behave like digital cooperatives.

Ethereum's upcoming upgrades continue to improve its speed and sustainability. It has become the backbone of decentralized applications, and it will likely remain a central hub for machine coordination in the future.

Solana – The Speed Layer

If Ethereum is the brain, Solana is the nervous system. It was built for speed and scale. Solana uses a unique system called Proof of History that allows it to process thousands of transactions per second at low cost (Yakovenko, 2020).

This makes it perfect for high-volume applications like gaming, DePINs, and real-time AI systems. Solana's design allows fast coordination between devices and users. It also supports projects like Render Network, which distributes GPU power for AI computing.

Solana has become one of the most important blockchains in the world because it proves that decentralized systems can be both fast and affordable.

Cardano – The Academic Blockchain

Cardano was born from research. Its creators used peer-reviewed papers and formal verification to build a network focused on long-term stability and global use (Hoskinson, 2020). It is designed for governments, education, and enterprise systems that need strong verification and low energy use.

Cardano also supports projects that link blockchain with artificial intelligence. It was one of the first to explore quantum-safe cryptography, which protects blockchains from future quantum computers. Its slow and careful growth model makes it a steady player in the world of serious infrastructure.

Avalanche – The Internet of Blockchains

Avalanche was built to connect many blockchains together. Its structure allows developers to create independent "subnets," which are smaller blockchains that still share the same core network (Ava Labs, 2024).

This modular design makes Avalanche ideal for machine learning and robotics projects that need specialized networks. For example, an AI company could run its own subnet that connects data, users, and compute nodes while still using Avalanche's main chain for security.

Avalanche is fast, efficient, and flexible. It shows that the blockchain world is not one single chain but a growing web of networks that can talk to each other.

Polkadot – The Great Connector

Polkadot is built around connection. It allows many blockchains, called parachains, to operate in harmony while sharing information through a secure central relay chain (Wood, 2020).

Polkadot acts as a bridge between different systems. It can connect Ethereum, Bitcoin sidechains, and new specialized networks. This makes it vital for the future of DePINs and the machine economy, where different networks will need to trade data, energy, and payments seamlessly.

Polkadot's vision is to create an internet of blockchains, a place where innovation is not limited by walls.

Cosmos – The Internet of Interoperability

Cosmos has a similar mission to Polkadot but approaches it differently. It focuses on interoperability—making sure different blockchains can talk to one another easily (Kwon, 2019). Its slogan is "the internet of blockchains."

Cosmos uses a system called the Inter-Blockchain Communication Protocol (IBC), which lets chains exchange data and tokens without going through a central hub. This structure makes Cosmos ideal for AI systems that depend on multiple data sources.

Cosmos represents freedom and flexibility, allowing hundreds of independent projects to thrive while still remaining part of a larger ecosystem.

Tezos – The Self-Updating Blockchain

Tezos introduced a simple but brilliant idea: a blockchain that can upgrade itself. Its community can vote on changes to the network, and once approved, those upgrades happen automatically without forks (Tezos Foundation, 2024).

This model keeps Tezos flexible and democratic. It is used in art markets, real estate, and digital identity systems. Its design makes it appealing to developers who value governance and smooth adaptation.

Tezos has also become popular in the AI and NFT community because it offers low fees and an environmentally friendly proof-of-stake model.

Chainlink – The Bridge Between Data and Code

Chainlink solves a vital problem in smart contracts. Most blockchains cannot access real-world data directly. Chainlink acts as a bridge, feeding external information—like prices, weather, or even sensor data—into blockchains safely (SmartContract, 2024).

Without Chainlink, smart contracts would be blind. With it, they can make intelligent decisions based on real events. This system is essential for DePINs and AI models that rely on accurate data.

Near Protocol – The Developer's Playground

Near is known for its simplicity and user-friendly design. It focuses on making blockchain development accessible to everyone (Near Foundation, 2024).

Its speed and low cost make it perfect for experiments in AI, Web3 apps, and educational systems. Near has positioned itself as a bridge between Web2 and Web3, helping traditional developers move into decentralized systems.

Algorand – Quantum Safe and Green

Algorand was created by MIT professor Silvio Micali, one of the inventors of zero-knowledge proofs. The network is designed to be secure, fast, and resistant to quantum attacks (Algorand Foundation, 2025).

Its low energy use and predictable performance make it a favorite for institutional projects and government use. Algorand is already being tested for digital identity, carbon tracking, and AI-driven logistics.

The deeper I studied the blockchain landscape, the more I realized that we are witnessing the birth of a planetary operating system. Each chain represents a different layer of intelligence. Some are thinkers, some are traders, some are builders. Together, they form the global backbone of digital value.

We began with the major blockchains that set the stage: Bitcoin, Ethereum, Solana, Cardano, Avalanche, Polkadot, Cosmos, Tezos, Chainlink, Near, and Algorand. Now let us continue the journey through the rest of the Top 50, the networks shaping the next generation of AI, quantum, and machine-based systems.

Aptos – The Precision Chain

Aptos was built by former engineers from Meta who wanted to create a blockchain that could handle millions of transactions without breaking (Aptos Foundation, 2024). It uses a programming language called Move, designed for safety and speed.

This makes Aptos useful for DePINs, gaming, and high-speed AI systems that depend on smooth communication. Its goal is to make blockchain performance feel invisible—fast, reliable, and seamless.

Sui – The Object-Oriented Chain

Sui also uses the Move language but focuses on digital ownership. It treats every piece of data as an object, allowing more flexible and complex applications (Sui Foundation, 2025).

Sui's structure makes it ideal for metaverse systems, NFTs, and AI-driven environments where every object can have identity and memory. It represents the future of smart assets—digital items that can think for themselves.

Arbitrum – Scaling Ethereum

Arbitrum helps Ethereum handle more transactions by running them off the main chain and then reporting the results back (Offchain Labs, 2024). This is called a Layer 2 network. It keeps costs low while keeping Ethereum's security.

AI models and decentralized apps benefit from this structure because they can move faster and cheaper without losing reliability. Arbitrum shows how optimization layers will help AI systems grow inside existing blockchains.

Optimism – The Human Layer

Optimism is another Layer 2 solution for Ethereum, but it focuses heavily on community and public good (Optimism Foundation, 2024). Its developers share revenue with builders and create systems for sustainable growth.

Optimism has become known for its fair design and open governance. This focus on community mirrors how open-source AI thrives—built by people who share knowledge and values.

Celestia – The Modular Chain

Celestia introduces a concept called modular blockchain architecture. Instead of doing everything itself, it separates tasks into layers: data availability, consensus, and execution (Celestia Labs, 2024).

This makes it flexible for AI and robotics projects that need custom blockchains without building from scratch. Think of Celestia as Lego blocks for blockchain developers. It represents the modular future of digital systems.

Kaspa – The Next Bitcoin Candidate

Kaspa is often called "the fastest proof-of-work blockchain." It improves on Bitcoin's design by allowing blocks to be processed in parallel, which means faster transactions without losing decentralization (Kaspa Community, 2025).

Kaspa is designed for speed, transparency, and fairness. It could become the next evolution of Bitcoin—a digital currency built for the machine era.

Ton (The Open Network) – The Social Chain

TON began inside Telegram, one of the world's biggest messaging apps. After regulatory delays, it became a community-led project. Today, TON connects payments, smart contracts, and communication directly inside social platforms (TON Foundation, 2025).

This integration means billions of users could one day access crypto tools without leaving their favorite apps. It is one of the few blockchains designed for mass adoption from day one.

Stellar – The Global Payments Network

Stellar was created to bring fast, low-cost payments to everyone on Earth (Stellar Foundation, 2024). Its mission is financial inclusion. Banks, fintech apps, and charities use Stellar to move money across borders in seconds.

Stellar also works on humanitarian blockchain projects like digital aid distribution and currency exchange. It connects human need with digital efficiency.

Ripple (XRP Ledger) – The Bridge for Banks

Ripple was one of the first blockchains to focus on banks and large financial institutions. It provides real-time cross-border payments that are faster and cheaper than the traditional SWIFT system (Ripple Labs, 2024).

While Ripple has faced regulatory battles, its technology continues to lead in enterprise finance. Many central banks study Ripple's model for digital currency frameworks.

Tron – The Digital Content Chain

Tron built its reputation by focusing on entertainment and media. It allows creators to share and monetize digital content directly without paying large platform fees (Tron Foundation, 2024).

Tron is used in gaming, streaming, and NFT projects. Its fast transactions and low fees make it ideal for high-volume creative industries. It represents how blockchain can empower artists and developers worldwide.

VeChain – The Supply Chain Specialist

VeChain brings transparency to logistics. It tracks goods through every step of the supply chain using blockchain records (VeChain Foundation, 2024).

This is vital for AI-driven industries like manufacturing and food safety, where accurate data prevents waste and fraud. VeChain's technology is already used by global brands for real-time quality control.

Hedera – The Enterprise Chain

Hedera uses a technology called Hashgraph, which processes transactions quickly and fairly without traditional blocks (Hedera Council, 2024).

It focuses on enterprise solutions, allowing businesses and governments to use blockchain safely. Hedera's governing council includes major global companies. Its speed and stability make it an attractive base for AI data management.

Flow – The Creator's Playground

Flow was built by Dapper Labs, the team behind NBA Top Shot. It is designed for games, NFTs, and digital experiences (Flow Foundation, 2024).

Flow proves that blockchain can power fun and accessible creativity. It is fast, low-cost, and developer-friendly. Many see it as the future of digital entertainment economies.

Internet Computer (ICP) – The Decentralized Cloud

ICP aims to replace traditional cloud computing with a decentralized alternative. It allows developers to run web apps directly on the blockchain without relying on Amazon or Google servers (DFINITY Foundation, 2024).

This is key for AI developers who want independence from centralized platforms. It also supports smart contracts that update in real time. ICP could become the internet's new foundation for autonomous applications.

Filecoin – The Storage Economy

Filecoin rewards people for sharing unused digital storage. Instead of relying on one company to hold all the world's data, it spreads it across a global network (Protocol Labs, 2024).

AI needs massive amounts of data. Filecoin gives it a home that is secure and community-powered. It is the digital warehouse of the future.

Arweave – The Permanent Internet

Arweave takes data storage even further. It lets users store files permanently. Once uploaded, data stays forever, supported by a unique economic model (Arweave Foundation, 2024).

This permanence makes Arweave a trusted archive for digital history and AI datasets. Nothing disappears, which is vital for transparent machine learning records.

Render Network – The Visual Engine

Render allows people to rent their unused graphics cards to create visuals and train AI models. It is the first major DePIN project that merges crypto with creative compute (Render Network Foundation, 2025).

Render makes digital creation more democratic. Anyone can contribute GPU power and earn tokens while helping artists and developers build the future.

Akash Network – The Open Cloud

Akash offers decentralized cloud computing. It lets users deploy apps and AI workloads across a distributed network instead of renting from big tech companies (Akash Network, 2025).

Akash supports the rise of decentralized AI. It is a critical piece of the infrastructure for the machine economy.

Bittensor – The AI Intelligence Network

Bittensor rewards people for training and sharing AI models on a decentralized platform (Bittensor Foundation, 2025).

It is one of the most advanced intersections of blockchain and machine learning. Every participant contributes intelligence to a shared network and gets rewarded for improving it.

This could be the blueprint for how AI and crypto grow together.

SingularityNET – The AI Marketplace

SingularityNET allows developers to sell and connect AI services through blockchain (SingularityNET Foundation, 2024).

It gives AI a global marketplace where algorithms can trade skills, connect, and cooperate. It represents the open-source dream of artificial general intelligence built by humanity, not owned by one company.

Ocean Protocol – The Data Exchange

Ocean Protocol makes data a liquid asset. It allows people to share and sell datasets securely through blockchain (Ocean Protocol Foundation, 2024).

This is vital for AI training. It creates a transparent market for data ownership while protecting privacy. Ocean turns data into fuel for the intelligence economy.

Fetch.ai – The Agent Economy

Fetch.ai focuses on autonomous economic agents—digital entities that can learn, negotiate, and act on behalf of humans (Fetch.ai, 2025).

It is one of the closest examples of AI and blockchain fully merging. Imagine millions of digital assistants trading energy, data, or services for you. That is the world Fetch is building.

IoTeX – The Internet of Trusted Things

IoTeX connects real-world devices through blockchain, allowing machines to verify and trade data directly (IoTeX Foundation, 2025).

It links robotics, sensors, and DePINs into a single ecosystem. IoTeX is where the physical and digital meet.

Helium – The People's Network

Helium lets people create a global wireless network by plugging in small hotspots that earn tokens (Helium Foundation, 2024).

It proved that communities can build telecom infrastructure without billion-dollar corporations. It is now expanding into 5G and IoT coverage worldwide.

Hivemapper – The Decentralized Map

Hivemapper rewards drivers for collecting map data with dash cameras (Hivemapper, 2024).

This system builds maps faster than traditional companies like Google. Every contributor owns a piece of the map, creating a fairer way to build global data systems.

WeatherXM – The Climate Chain

WeatherXM pays people to operate weather stations that collect real-time climate data (WeatherXM, 2025).

AI models use that data to predict weather and manage agriculture. It is a real-world DePIN that turns data collection into a shared business.

Energy Web – The Green Grid

Energy Web helps utilities and renewable energy projects manage power through blockchain (Energy Web Foundation, 2024).

This network allows homes, cars, and solar panels to trade energy automatically. It is how AI will balance the power grid of the future.

VeWorld, Oasis, Starknet, Zilliqa, Celo, and Beyond

The blockchain world is vast and still growing. Each of these emerging chains focuses on privacy, scaling, or sustainability. Together, they complete the picture of a living digital planet made of thousands of connected networks.

When you study these blockchains, you see a pattern. They are not separate projects. They are cells in one digital organism. Each chain does a job; storage, compute, data, or trust. Together, they form the foundation of the next economy, where humans and machines collaborate in real time.

This is why I believe the blockchain is not just a technology. It is an evolution of coordination. It is how we teach machines to be honest, how we teach data to belong, and how we teach the digital world to work for everyone.

6

Bitcoin and the Search for the Next Bitcoin

1. **Why Bitcoin Still Matters**

When I look at the ecosystem today, I keep coming back to one truth: Bitcoin matters. It was the first blockchain to prove that a decentralized, permissionless, cryptographic digital asset could store value

In the machine economy we've been walking through, value isn't just money; it's trust, coordination, record-keeping, and the ledger of machine actions. Bitcoin remains the strongest base layer of trust.

Because of that, even as AI, quantum computing, DePINs and new architectures rise, you still want to understand what makes "the next Bitcoin" meaningful: a very large network effect, deep trust in the protocol, defensible scarcity or utility, and a role in the machine economy beyond speculation.

2. **What Could "Next Bitcoin" Mean?**

Here are criteria I use to judge potential candidates:

- Strong-chain security and decentralisation: Without trust, nothing else works.
- Large address base, widespread adoption, developer ecosystem: The more nodes, users and apps, the stronger the network.
- Utility aligned with the machine economy: It must power things machines need—data, compute, consensus, identities, devices, etc.
- Tokenomics that support adoption and growth: Not just hype but real incentives, usage, governance, sustainability.
- Scalability and adjustability: The protocol must evolve as demands rise.
- Bridge to real-world systems: Whether that means IoT devices, sensors, robots, AI agents paying each other, or infrastructure networks.

3. **Strong Candidates for "Next Bitcoin"**

Based on those criteria, I've identified a few chains that carry high probability for being major pillars of the machine economy; possibly rising to the stature of Bitcoin, though not guaranteed.

a) **Solana (SOL)**

Solana stands out for speed and cost efficiency. It has smart-contract capability, high throughput, and is increasingly used in DeFi, NFTs, and layers that support machine workflows.

With regulatory tailwinds (for example, as alt-coins near ETF candidacy) it gets extra legitimacy.

In the machine economy scenario, Solana could serve as the real-time execution layer for machines, AI agents, DePIN networks and sensors exchanging value and data quickly.

b) **Kaspa (KAS)**

Kaspa is less talked about but interesting: built on Proof-of-Work with parallel chain design, faster blocks, decentralisation, and next-generation throughput.

If machines are doing constant small transactions—sensors paying gateways, devices renting compute—Kaspa's design could handle that micro-economy better than legacy chains.

It ticks many boxes: scalability, trust, decentralisation, niche utility for machine economy.

c) **Algorand (ALGO)**

Algorand is worth highlighting because of its focus on efficient, quantum-safe cryptography and institutional use-cases.

In a future where quantum computers threaten older cryptos, Algorand's positioning gives it an edge. And in the machine economy, large institutions, identity systems, real-world assets and AI may prefer a chain with that security profile.

d) **Bonus: Bitcoin (BTC) Itself**

Don't forget: Bitcoin might still evolve. It might take on new roles (e.g., strategic reserve, base layer for machine payments) rather than be "the next Bitcoin."

So a candidate for "next Bitcoin" doesn't necessarily mean replacing Bitcoin but standing alongside or supporting it in a shifted ecosystem.

4. **Stocks to Watch: The Bridge Between Crypto, AI & Hardware**

Now shifting to stocks; because you asked for high-probability stocks that align with AI, ML, quantum, blockchain and the machine economy. These are companies I believe have structural advantage.

a) **NVIDIA Corporation (NVDA)**

Nvidia is central in AI chips, GPUs, training of large language models and data-centres. Its dominance gives it massive leverage into any infrastructure build-out for machines, blockchains and autonomy.

In our machine economy map: compute = power. Nvidia provides that power.

b) **Taiwan Semiconductor Manufacturing Company (TSMC)**

TSMC may not be a flashy "crypto stock" but in the compute chain it is foundational. AI and blockchain both demand advanced semiconductors. TSMC supplies chips across that spectrum.

c) **Broadcom Inc. (AVGO)**

Broadcom is interesting because of its custom ASIC and AI-chip work, positioning in next-gen computing and infrastructure for AI and blockchain workloads.

d) **Advanced Micro Devices, Inc. (AMD)**

AMD competes in GPUs/CPUs and increasingly is part of the distributed compute and machine economy infrastructure. It benefits from AI growth and blockchain compute demand.

e) **Palantir Technologies Inc. (PLTR)**

Palantir is a data analytics company bridging AI and real-world systems, government and enterprise. Blockchain + machine economy = data + trust +

infrastructure. Palantir sits well in that mix.

5. **Risks & What Could Break the Thesis**

This is where we get real. For any of these candidates to succeed, certain things must line up; and several things could block the path.

Regulation & legality: Crypto remains under regulatory threat. Chains that become too centralised, or that break rules, may fail.

Network security failures: A major exploit or loss of decentralisation could kill trust.

Utility-failure: If machines don't adopt these chains, or DePINs don't scale as expected, the network effect fizzles.

Competition / technological obsolescence: Blockchain is evolving fast. A newer chain with better utility could leapfrog these candidates.

Hardware supply / geopolitical constraints: Stocks like Nvidia or TSMC depend on supply chains, trade, and manufacturing.

Macro / sentiment risk: Crypto markets are highly volatile. Stocks too can be hit by broader market drops in tech.

6. **My Highest-Probability Path Forward**

Based on everything, here is my "most likely scenario" for where value flows in the machine economy over the next 3-5 years.

Bitcoin remains base layer store of value and trust.

Solana becomes a major operational layer for AI-agent, DePIN, machine-to-machine value flows; this gives it "next Bitcoin" type importance.

Kaspa emerges or grows significantly as a high-throughput, decentralised chain focusing on machine micro-transactions.

Algorand plays the institutional and quantum-safe role.

On the stock side: Nvidia and TSMC dominate compute hardware; Broadcom and AMD fill the infrastructure and custom chip slots; Palantir links data, AI and systems integration.

These flows reinforce each other: machines rent compute, machines pay on chains, chains record trust, chips power the system. It becomes a virtuous cycle around the machine economy.

7. **What To Watch (Signals)**

Here are some specific signs I'll be looking for as I track this thesis:

- Big partnerships between chains and machine/robotics firms (e.g., DePIN networks choosing Solana or Kaspa).
- Surge in on-chain machine payments (e.g., IoT devices paying for services).
- Regulatory recognition of chains as infrastructure (e.g., potential ETFs or institutional adoption).
- Chip companies reporting compute demand from crypto/blockchain mining or machine economy workloads.
- Security proofs, quantum-safe upgrades, weave-in of AI agent marketplaces on chains.

In this chapter I wanted to show you how to think about the "next Bitcoin" in the context of the machine economy. It is not about which coin doubles next week. It is about which chains and companies become foundational infrastructure for the intelligent machine layer of our world.

If you follow compute, data, trust and real-world machine value flows, a map emerges. And if you believe (as I do) that the machine economy is coming, then **Solana, Kaspa, Algorand** and the handful of hardware/AI stocks we listed are not wild bets. They are informed plays on the next era.

Stay curious. Stay critical. I'll keep watching what unfolds. The machine economy is not a coming wave; it's already rising.

7

Smart Contracts and Machine Logic

When I first learned about smart contracts, I realized they were more than computer code. They were digital promises. A smart contract is a small program that runs itself once certain conditions are met. No lawyers, no waiting, no middleman. Once it starts, it finishes. That single idea changes everything about how humans and machines interact.

1. From Paper Contracts to Machine Logic

For thousands of years, humans have made agreements with words, signatures, and trust. We wrote contracts on paper and hoped both sides would keep their word. Smart contracts replace that fragile trust with math. Once deployed on a blockchain, the rules cannot be changed. The code enforces the promise.

Think about it: when a car rental app uses a smart contract, payment happens automatically when conditions are met. The customer receives the car key as soon as the blockchain verifies payment. There is no delay, no clerk, and no dispute. The system simply runs.

That same logic can apply to AI agents, robots, and entire industries. Machines can use smart contracts to pay for data, power, or maintenance without human input. The blockchain acts as both accountant and referee.

2. How Smart Contracts Work

Smart contracts live on blockchains such as Ethereum, Solana, Cardano, and Avalanche. Developers write them in code languages like Solidity or Rust. Once uploaded to the blockchain, they cannot be edited. The contract waits for inputs—such as a payment, a sensor reading, or a digital signature—and then performs an action.

Each action becomes part of the permanent ledger. That record builds trust among users and machines alike. If two robots trade energy or data through a smart contract, the blockchain ensures both sides get exactly what they agreed to.

This concept is already alive in decentralized finance (DeFi). Automated exchanges use smart contracts to swap assets without banks. In DePINs, smart contracts handle network rewards, confirming who contributed computing power or bandwidth. In the machine economy, these same contracts will manage billions of micro-transactions every day.

3. AI and the Rise of Self-Running Systems

As artificial intelligence grows, smart contracts become its hands. They give AI the ability to act in the real world. A model can learn, plan, and make predictions, but it needs a trusted system to carry out decisions. That is what blockchains provide.

Imagine an AI farm manager that monitors weather and soil data. When rain is coming, it triggers a smart contract that pays drones to fertilize or irrigate the field. The drones record proof of work on the blockchain, and the AI releases payment instantly. No supervision. No delay.

This is not science fiction. Projects like Fetch.ai and Ocean Protocol are already testing similar systems. Fetch.ai allows AI agents to negotiate and trade services automatically. Ocean Protocol uses blockchain to manage data rights and automate payments when that data is used (Fetch.ai, 2025; Ocean Protocol Foundation, 2024).

When these tools mature, we will see self-running supply chains, fleets of delivery bots, and smart cities that balance power grids in real time. Each machine will act within the boundaries of its smart contracts, ensuring order and fairness.

4. The Language of the Machine Economy

In this new world, code becomes law. But unlike human law, machine law executes perfectly every time.

Smart contracts bring a new kind of clarity to business. Payments settle instantly. Ownership transfers automatically. Records cannot be erased. Machines can read, verify, and execute everything themselves.

The more AI systems evolve, the more they will depend on this structure. Humans will design goals, but smart contracts will handle the transactions and enforcement. This is how global coordination becomes possible without chaos.

5. Limitations and Lessons

Smart contracts are powerful but not magic. They only know what is on the blockchain. They cannot access outside information on their own. This is where oracles come in—systems like Chainlink that bring real-world data into the chain safely (SmartContract, 2024). Oracles allow smart contracts to respond to prices, weather, or even machine sensor readings.

Another challenge is human error. Code can contain bugs. Once deployed, mistakes cannot be undone easily. That is why careful testing and formal verification are essential. The success of the machine economy will depend on trustworthy code written by ethical developers.

Security also matters. If someone manipulates an oracle or exploits a contract's weakness, entire systems can fail. The blockchain may be secure, but the code that runs on it must be just as strong.

These lessons remind us that technology does not replace responsibility. It only amplifies it.

6. The Future: Contracts Between Minds

As AI grows more capable, smart contracts will become its natural habitat. Imagine two AI systems negotiating a deal: one sells renewable energy data, the other buys it to optimize electric vehicles. They agree on price, confirm delivery, and close the deal—all through a blockchain contract.

This is where the machine economy begins to resemble a living organism. Each node acts independently but cooperates through shared logic.

We are moving toward a future where machine logic becomes part of daily life. Cars will buy their own insurance. Homes will pay for power in real time. Robots will negotiate repair services with each other. Humans will oversee the big picture while machines handle the details.

At the center of all this are smart contracts, quiet and tireless, writing the laws of the digital world one block at a time.

7. Invest AI Takeaways

When I look back at history, I see patterns. The printing press automated knowledge. The internet automated communication. Blockchain and smart contracts automate trust.

This evolution means we can build economies that run on honesty, not control. In the past, systems required banks, middlemen, and gatekeepers. The new world runs on verified code.

This technology gives small creators, small businesses, and even individual machines the same access to global markets as large institutions. It levels the playing field in ways that humanity has never seen.

For me, that is what makes this chapter important. Smart contracts are not just a tool. They are a new form of social contract, written in code and powered by collective trust.

8

Meme Coins and the Energy of Culture: Top 20 Meme Coins with Potential

SPECIAL MEME COIN DISCLAIMER

The section on meme coins and cultural tokens is included only for educational and creative understanding. It is meant to explain how meme coins function in culture and technology. It does not encourage, promote, or recommend the creation, purchase, or trading of any specific token or cryptocurrency.

Meme coins are extremely speculative digital assets that can experience rapid and unpredictable price swings. Many projects have no proven fundamentals, no long-term vision, and no regulatory protection. Anyone who trades or invests in meme coins does so entirely at their own risk.

Readers should use careful judgment, perform thorough independent research, and seek professional financial advice before taking part in any cryptocurrency project. The purpose of this chapter is to help readers understand how creativity, community, and innovation intersect in the digital economy. It is not designed to provide or imply investment advice of any kind.

When I first entered the crypto world, I ignored meme coins. I thought they were jokes. Then I watched Dogecoin grow into a global movement and realized something important. Meme coins are not only about speculation. They are about energy. They reflect the collective power of attention. If Bitcoin is digital gold, meme coins are digital culture. They show how human creativity can turn emotion into value. When that emotional energy combines with artificial intelligence and social media, it becomes one of the most powerful forces in modern finance.

Every market runs on emotion. People buy because they believe in a story. Meme coins take that truth and turn it into a feature. They are social tokens that capture humor, rebellion, and imagination. When you see a meme coin with a wild name or a funny logo, what you are really seeing is a crowd's heartbeat. Each share, tweet, or post amplifies that pulse. The blockchain records the transactions, but the real fuel is culture.

Artificial intelligence makes this even more dynamic. Language models and image generators can now create infinite memes, stories, and personalities around a coin. The marketing is automated and the creativity is endless. That is why meme coins spread faster than traditional investments. They feed on emotion and move at digital speed.

Dogecoin was the first to prove this idea. Created in 2013 as a joke, it became one of the most traded cryptocurrencies in the world. Its mascot, a smiling Shiba Inu dog, represented the internet's love for irony and positivity (Dogecoin Foundation, 2024). What made Dogecoin special was not its code but its community. People used it for tipping, charity, and fun. It reminded everyone that money could also be joyful. In the age of the machine economy, Dogecoin's simplicity and speed make it useful again. As bots and digital agents become more common, lightweight coins like Dogecoin could become their preferred currency for microtransactions.

After Dogecoin came Shiba Inu, Pepe, and a wave of new meme ecosystems. Shiba Inu called itself the "Dogecoin killer," but its true innovation was community-driven growth. It built its own exchange, ShibaSwap, and its own Layer 2 blockchain, Shibarium, to lower transaction costs (Shiba Inu Ecosystem, 2025). Pepe followed in 2023 and exploded in volume within days. Based on a popular internet frog meme, it showed how fast viral culture could move markets. These projects are unpredictable, yet they reveal something deep about modern finance. People crave belonging. They want to feel part of something alive. Meme coins give them that sense of connection through humor and shared identity.

The machine economy may run on data and compute power, but it also runs on stories. Humans give machines meaning through culture, and meme coins prove that imagination has economic value. They are the emotional layer of blockchain. They measure participation as much as productivity. Every post, every meme, every moment of attention becomes a small vote of belief, and the blockchain keeps score. Artificial intelligence can now read these signals. It can track social trends, detect viral spikes, and predict which tokens might rise based on online behavior. Meme coins are no longer random. They are signals of collective attention, and AI can both measure and amplify them.

In 2024 and 2025, the next phase of meme coins began to emerge. Some were entirely designed by AI. Others used AI to manage marketing, automate community updates, or even optimize token trading. One project, Turbo, famously used ChatGPT to design its entire launch. Another, AIDOGE, combined meme branding with AI generation (Turbo AI Project, 2024; AIDOGE Network, 2024). These hybrid tokens blur the line between humor, creativity, and computation. AI can simulate what makes a meme viral, test names, logos, and narratives in real time, and adjust based on engagement. The result is a chaotic but fascinating ecosystem where human creativity and machine learning constantly remix each other.

From an investment perspective, meme coins matter not because they are stable, but because they reveal where attention flows. They are lightning in digital form. You cannot hold it, but you can watch where it strikes. Meme coins show how digital tribes form and how culture moves before capital does. When the world rallies around an idea, even a silly one, it often signals a deeper trend. That energy frequently spills over into more serious innovations and real technologies. Many developers who started with memes later created useful tools, exchanges, and decentralized applications. That is the hidden power of meme culture. It recruits creativity into technology.

I believe we are entering a new phase of digital culture where AI will not just help create meme coins, but become part of their identity. Imagine AI-generated characters that evolve over time, each backed by its own token. Fans could own pieces of those living digital beings. These character coins could form the entertainment industry of the blockchain era. Music, art, gaming, and storytelling could merge into living ecosystems powered by both community and computation. Meme coins will continue to evolve into full cultural networks, blending art, AI, and imagination. They remind us that money is a story we tell together, and sometimes the funniest stories are the ones that change the world.

Over the last few years I have learned that attention is a resource, and whoever can gather it can create value. Community is capital, because a passionate crowd can move faster than a corporation. Artificial intelligence accelerates creativity, turning the internet into a global idea generator. Culture always leads technology, because before innovation can scale, people must first feel it. Meme coins are not the core of finance, but they are the pulse that pushes finance forward. When you mix intelligence, creativity, and emotion, you get a new form of power. And in the next chapter, we will see how that power meets quantum computing—the final frontier where data, trust, and speed collide.

Top 20 Meme Coins with Potential

Below are twenty meme-based or meme-adjacent cryptocurrencies that currently have community energy, public visibility, or experimental potential. None of these are recommendations, but each reflects a cultural signal worth studying.

Dogecoin (DOGE) remains the original internet coin, famous for its humor, speed, and loyal community. Shiba Inu (SHIB) evolved beyond its meme roots with its Shibarium network. Pepe (PEPE) showed how fast a viral trend can become a market force. Bonk (BONK) on Solana represents how meme culture can merge with ecosystem airdrops. Floki Inu (FLOKI) continues to blend NFTs, gaming, and branding into a more complex network. Dogelon Mars (ELON) thrives on space-themed humor and social traction. Popcat (POPCAT) and Dogwifhat (WIF) reflect the rising Solana meme wave, where energy comes from community-driven hype. The $TRUMP coin represents politically charged memes and volatility, while Gigachad (GIGA) and Snek (SNEK) thrive on internet irony. Non-Playable Coin (NPC) and Just a Chill Guy (CHILLGUY) push humor as identity. Fartcoin (FARTCOIN) and Moo Deng (MOODENG) show how absurdity itself can drive value. Troller Cat (TCAT) and SPX6900 (SPX) represent newer experiments in meme-based branding. Finally, Ape, Happy Coin, and Act I are examples of smaller meme projects that may evolve into creative ecosystems if their communities stay active.

All of these tokens share a few traits. They rise through attention and community engagement rather than fundamental value. They can crash quickly, but they can also act as early indicators of where internet culture is headed. The lesson is to observe, not chase. Meme coins teach us that participation itself has power, and culture is often the first signal of economic change.

9

How to Build a Meme Coin That Matters

SPECIAL MEME COIN DISCLAIMER

The section on meme coins and cultural tokens is included only for educational and creative understanding. It is meant to explain how meme coins function in culture and technology. It does not encourage, promote, or recommend the creation, purchase, or trading of any specific token or cryptocurrency.

Meme coins are extremely speculative digital assets that can experience rapid and unpredictable price swings. Many projects have no proven fundamentals, no long-term vision, and no regulatory protection. Anyone who trades or invests in meme coins does so entirely at their own risk.

Readers should use careful judgment, perform thorough independent research, and seek professional financial advice before taking part in any cryptocurrency project. The purpose of this chapter is to help readers understand how creativity, community, and innovation intersect in the digital economy. It is not designed to provide or imply investment advice of any kind.

When I first started studying meme coins, I thought they were all hype. I saw them as jokes that came and went with the mood of the internet. But over time, I began to understand something more powerful. Meme coins are not just digital jokes anymore. They are proof that people want to belong to something greater than themselves. They show that culture itself can create value.

This chapter is about how a meme coin can evolve into something that lasts, something that means more than money. It is about how creativity, community, and purpose can shape a digital project that lives and grows inside the machine economy. The principles here apply whether you are an artist, a coder, or a visionary who wants to connect people through shared meaning.

Every great meme coin starts with humor. Humor disarms people and builds connection. It is simple and human. But a joke becomes a movement only when it touches something real. Dogecoin proved this first. What began as a parody of Bitcoin became a culture of kindness and generosity. Its joyful tone and positive spirit drew millions of believers into one of the largest communities in crypto (Dogecoin Foundation, 2024). Shiba Inu followed with the idea of a "decentralized community movement." It took the meme format and turned it into a brand that lives on multiple platforms with its own blockchain ecosystem. Both coins remind us that the story behind a project is its soul. A meme coin that matters must say something true about how people feel.

Before you write any code or design a logo, ask yourself what your coin stands for. A meme coin without purpose is just noise. The best ones speak to shared values or causes that people care about. Maybe your project celebrates creativity, supports clean energy, or funds DePIN networks that help communities share power and data. Purpose turns curiosity into loyalty. It turns holders into believers.

A meme coin does not start with the token. It starts with the people. Your community is your company, your marketing team, and your investors. Build your people before you build your product. Open a space for conversation. Share your idea, listen to feedback, and let humor be your bridge. When people feel included, they become your first advocates. The early members should feel like pioneers in a cultural movement, not just customers waiting for a price to rise.

Once your vision and community are alive, it is time to shape your tokenomics. Tokenomics is the design of how your coin lives, moves, and rewards participation. Many meme coins fail here because they create too many tokens or give too much to insiders, breaking trust before the project even begins. Keep your supply simple and transparent. Make it clear how tokens are created, distributed, and burned. Lock liquidity pools and make everything public. Never promise profits. Focus on participation. People can forgive a bad week in the market, but they never forgive hidden rules.

Utility is what keeps a meme coin alive after the laughter fades. A coin that does something real will always outlast one that only entertains. Give your holders reasons to use their tokens beyond speculation. A coin could grant access to exclusive content or digital art. It could act as payment inside a game or reward people for contributing to DePIN systems. It could let the community vote on future updates or support artists through microgrants. The goal is to make your token useful, not just valuable. If people can use it, they will keep it.

Choosing the right blockchain is the next major step. Ethereum remains the most flexible platform for smart contracts and community-driven projects. Solana is faster and cheaper, which is helpful for DePIN systems and small transactions. Binance Smart Chain offers low fees and wide access. Polygon is lightweight and eco-friendly, a strong choice for gaming and NFTs (Polygon Labs, 2025). The best chain for you depends on your purpose. If your project involves AI or high-frequency interactions, Solana or Polygon might be ideal. If you want deep customization and governance tools, Ethereum is hard to beat. Whatever you choose, prioritize security. Hire auditors, test your contracts, and never rush your launch.

When launch day comes, remember that you are launching a story, not a stock. The people who join you should feel excitement, not pressure. Share your mission clearly and reward creativity over greed. Offer fair airdrops and let early members feel ownership. Never fake scarcity or create fear of missing out. Honesty builds stronger momentum than hype. Continue communicating after launch. Admit mistakes and celebrate progress. The projects that endure are the ones that keep showing up with authenticity.

Once your community is strong, start creating small ecosystems of utility. You can launch NFT collections, games, or creative tools that integrate your token. Partner with AI projects that need microtransactions. These experiments give your coin purpose. Over time, your meme coin can become a hybrid ecosystem of culture, technology, and community. Keep evolving, even if progress is slow. Every new use case strengthens your foundation.

Legal and ethical transparency are non-negotiable. Every country treats tokens differently, and ignorance will not protect you. If your coin does not represent a security, state that clearly. If you raise funds, disclose everything. Publish audits and keep a public wallet for all project funds. Work with advisors who understand digital law. Trust grows when you operate in the open. Your goal should never be to get rich fast. It should be to build something meaningful that can survive change and inspire others.

When you study the meme coins that lasted, you start to see the same DNA repeating. They all have purpose. They all have transparent systems. They all reward participation. They all create joy. And they all evolve. They lead with honesty, humor, and heart. Those are the ingredients of longevity.

Meme coins matter because they remind us of something essential. They show that technology is a tool, but people are the source of value. Even in a world shaped by artificial intelligence, it is still human creativity that gives meaning to code. The best projects of the next decade will combine intelligence with imagination. They will use memes to move culture and blockchains to preserve it.

The future of meme coins will be more serious than it sounds. They will power art economies, fund AI collaborations, and reward communities that share data and ideas. They will connect emotional energy with financial systems in a way that no other technology can. If we build with integrity and creativity, meme coins will become a form of digital folklore, proof that humor and heart still belong at the center of innovation.

The truth is that every meme coin carries a simple message. People want to belong. They want to believe in something. And when technology honors that need instead of exploiting it, it becomes timeless. A meme coin that matters does not chase profit. It builds culture. And culture, when cared for, always outlasts markets.

10

The Quantum Question

Every time I write about the future one word keeps returning to me, quantum. It sounds mysterious but it simply means small, so small that the usual rules of physics stop working. In that strange world particles can exist in two places at once and outcomes appear as probabilities instead of certainties. Quantum computing uses that strangeness to solve problems that ordinary computers cannot. Instead of bits that are either zero or one, quantum computers use qubits that can be both at the same time. That dual state makes them powerful and also dangerous because the same technology that can model the universe might one day break the encryption that protects our digital world. That is the quantum question, how do we build a future strong enough to survive the power of infinite computation.

A normal computer is like a light switch that can be on or off, but a quantum computer is like a dimmer knob that can hold every level of brightness at once. When many qubits combine the number of possible outcomes grows beyond imagination and even a small quantum computer can test more solutions in seconds than classical machines could in centuries. This power is ideal for science, chemistry, and artificial intelligence because quantum computers can model molecules, weather systems, and neural networks with precision that no classical computer can match. They can also search massive databases in seconds, yet that same power threatens one of the core foundations of digital security, encryption.

Blockchains depend on cryptographic puzzles that take time and energy to solve. These puzzles protect wallets, transactions, and smart contracts, but quantum computers could one day solve those puzzles almost instantly. Imagine a world where someone could guess private keys in seconds and every blockchain would be exposed. Bitcoin, Ethereum, and every other network would need a new kind of protection. This is not about fear but about readiness. Researchers around the world are developing what they call post-quantum cryptography, new mathematical systems built to resist quantum attacks (National Institute of Standards and Technology, 2025). Projects such as Algorand and Cardano are already testing quantum-resistant designs (Algorand Foundation, 2025). This effort may become one of the most important races in modern technology, the race to preserve digital trust before quantum computation reaches full scale.

Quantum computing is not only a threat, it is also an opportunity for the next phase of the machine economy. The same power that could break codes can also build faster, smarter, and cleaner systems. Artificial intelligence models that take days to train on classical hardware could one day train in minutes on quantum systems. Logistics networks, climate models, and genetic research could all become faster and more precise. Quantum computing could even improve blockchain itself because every blockchain relies on randomness to create secure keys and fair outcomes, and quantum systems can generate true randomness since the quantum world is inherently unpredictable. That property could make future blockchains even more secure.

When I think about the machine economy with robots, AI agents, and decentralized networks trading data and energy, I see quantum computing as both engine and shield. It could allow real-time optimization of logistics, energy grids, and communication systems while protecting those same systems with quantum-safe encryption. Imagine autonomous cars, delivery drones, and industrial robots communicating through quantum-encrypted channels where every move, transaction, and byte of data is protected from the fastest possible attack. The same power that can destroy trust can also rebuild it stronger, and that is the balance we must reach.

Some blockchains are already preparing for this future. Algorand was designed for cryptographic efficiency and is exploring quantum-safe upgrades. Cardano researchers are studying lattice-based cryptography, a method believed to resist quantum attacks. Ethereum developers are planning updates to include these algorithms once they are standardized, and even Bitcoin can evolve through small upgrades called soft forks to replace vulnerable systems. The first blockchains that adapt to the quantum era will likely become the most trusted digital systems on Earth.

Quantum computing is still young but several companies are already shaping its direction. IBM is an early pioneer offering a cloud-based quantum network for developers. Google reached what it called quantum supremacy in 2019 when its Sycamore processor solved a problem faster than any classical computer. IonQ specializes in trapped-ion quantum computers known for their stability. Rigetti Computing focuses on hybrid quantum-classical models that combine both strengths. D-Wave uses quantum annealing for optimization. These companies form the hardware layer of the quantum future and will play the same role for quantum computing that NVIDIA and TSMC play for artificial intelligence.

Every great leap in technology raises moral questions and quantum computing is no exception. When machines can simulate every possibility secrecy itself may disappear. Finance, privacy, and national security will all change. That is why the race to quantum safety is about more than algorithms, it is about values. We must decide how to use this power, whether to control or to create, to dominate or to protect. The answer will define the future of trust.

Quantum computing may take ten or twenty years to reach maturity but that time will come faster than we think. The wise path is to build systems that can evolve. Every blockchain, every AI framework, and every decentralized network should assume that quantum computing will one day arrive. That means designing adaptable protocols, supporting open research, and creating clear plans for secure transitions. The people and companies that prepare today will lead tomorrow while those who ignore the change may wake up to a world that moved without them.

When people hear about quantum technology their first response is often fear, and that is understandable, but every great discovery begins as something we do not fully understand. Quantum computing is not the end of blockchain, it is its next evolution. The future we are building depends on both truth and imagination. Quantum physics shows us that reality itself is full of possibilities, and blockchain teaches us that truth can be written and verified. Together they form a partnership between uncertainty and order.

The quantum question is not a warning but an invitation. The same power that can break codes can also break limits. If we approach it with wisdom and integrity quantum technology can unlock a world where trust, intelligence, and creativity exist in perfect balance.

11

The Future: When Machines Earn Too

I remember the first time I heard someone say that machines would one day earn their own money. It sounded strange, almost like science fiction. Yet it is already happening. Every time a robot runs on artificial intelligence, every time a sensor uploads data, and every time a DePIN node sends a reward, the machine is earning. The future is learning how to pay itself.

To understand what this means, picture a self-driving car. It is not just a vehicle. It is a computer on wheels with cameras, sensors, and software that collect information about roads, traffic, and energy use. That data has real value. With blockchain technology, the car can record and sell that data automatically. It can pay for charging, electricity, or tolls through its own digital wallet. The driver may still own it, but the car operates in its own small economy. The same idea applies to drones, smart homes, and industrial robots. Each one can join a network that earns, pays, and reports without a middleman. That is when the internet truly becomes alive with value.

This new machine economy already exists in small ways. It lives inside systems like Helium and Render, where machines and people share resources and get rewarded for participation. Over time, it will grow far larger. Artificial intelligence models will negotiate with one another for computing power. Robots will rent cloud services from decentralized networks. Smart factories will trade clean energy with local solar grids. Each exchange may be tiny, just a fraction of a cent, but billions of them will happen every second. Together, they will create a new kind of global economy, a machine economy.

Many people worry that when machines start earning, humans will lose their place. I see it differently. We will move from repetitive labor to designing, supervising, and guiding intelligent systems. Our role will be rooted in creativity, ethics, and direction. We will decide what the machines build and how they serve the world. This shift will create new types of work—robot trainers, AI negotiators, digital ethicists, and architects of the machine economy. The goal is not to compete with machines, but to work with them.

None of this is possible without trust. Machines can only cooperate if they can verify what others have done. That is what blockchain provides. Every payment, data exchange, and service record becomes part of a shared ledger. The blockchain becomes the nervous system of this new economy, connecting billions of devices at once. This is why crypto, artificial intelligence, and robotics are not separate movements. They are pieces of one system. Crypto records. AI thinks. Robotics acts. Together they form intelligence that can move, earn, and remember.

The hardware foundation behind this is critical. The chips, processors, and graphics units created by companies like NVIDIA, AMD, TSMC, and IBM are what make this intelligence possible. Every AI model and blockchain node depends on power and silicon. Every sensor needs a stable connection. Hardware is the body. Software is the brain. Blockchain is the memory. Investors who understand that connection will see where real value flows—not just in tokens, but in the companies that build the systems making all of this work.

Machine-to-machine trade is already becoming real. Tesla cars send data to servers and receive updates. Smart thermostats buy electricity at cheaper hours. Industrial robots order parts before they break. Smart contracts make this automatic. The contract sets the rule, the blockchain confirms the result, and the payment moves instantly. Imagine a world where your refrigerator orders groceries, your house rents spare battery power to the grid, and your AI assistant sells unused storage overnight. This is not fantasy. It is the next phase of logistics written in code.

The question then becomes what money machines will use. It might not be Bitcoin or dollars. It will likely be new digital currencies designed for speed and fairness. Projects like Solana, Kaspa, and Algorand already show how fast and secure payments can work for this purpose. In time, even central banks may issue special digital currencies for machine use, built to communicate directly with AI systems. The border between finance and infrastructure will disappear.

When machines begin to earn, they also begin to decide. That kind of power must come with accountability. We will need clear systems that prevent abuse, protect privacy, and keep humans in control. Every robot wallet should have an owner, and every autonomous contract must include human oversight. The more we delegate to machines, the more we must define our values in code. Ethics will not be an afterthought. It will be the foundation of trust.

If we do this carefully, the machine economy will not replace us. It will free us. Imagine a world where machines handle the hardest work, energy is clean, and money flows directly to where it is needed. People will have more time to create, learn, and connect. The blockchain ensures fairness, AI provides intelligence, and machines handle the scale. Humanity provides vision. This is not a dream. It is a path toward shared prosperity if we remain curious, thoughtful, and ethical.

In the years ahead, countless small signals and invisible payments will flow all around us. Machines will speak a new financial language made of data and trust. Quantum computers will power their choices. Blockchains will store their memories. DePIN networks will anchor them in the physical world. Through it all, humans will remain the storytellers; the ones who give meaning to the math.

That is what this book has been building toward: a clear understanding of the systems shaping our next chapter as a species. We are entering an age where intelligence exists everywhere, value is shared between humans and machines, and trust is written in code. This is the new economy. And it is already awake.

12

Decentralized AI: The Intelligence Layer of the Blockchain

The world is entering an age where artificial intelligence is no longer just software that serves humans. It is starting to function as an economic participant. Machines are learning to trade, pay for data, and even earn income for the work they perform. The intelligence that once lived in isolated data centers is now spreading across decentralized networks. It is learning to live on the blockchain.

In this chapter we explore the next layer of the digital economy, the one that sits above the hardware and the blockchain base. This layer is made of intelligence itself. It is where computation, data, and machine learning models interact in real time. This is what we call decentralized AI. It is the part of the crypto ecosystem that gives machines a mind of their own and lets them act inside the financial system.

The most exciting thing about this shift is that investors can now take part in it directly. Just as early blockchain investors once bought pieces of the network through coins like Bitcoin or Ethereum, we can now buy pieces of artificial intelligence through AI tokens. Each of these projects represents a small part of a living intelligence economy.

Bittensor, known by its symbol TAO, is one of the leaders in this space. It allows anyone in the world to contribute computing power or machine learning models and earn rewards when others use them. It is a network that pays for intelligence. Fetch AI creates small autonomous agents that can make decisions, book services, or exchange data without human oversight. Render lets people rent their unused graphics processing power to help AI artists, designers, and robotics researchers generate visuals. Akash provides decentralized cloud computing where any developer can rent or supply computing resources without relying on major corporations. Ocean Protocol gives AI developers access to open data marketplaces so that algorithms can train safely and fairly. Together these projects form the backbone of the decentralized AI stack. Compute, data, and intelligence now exist as separate but connected layers.

From an investment standpoint, these tokens are the next logical step after the DePIN networks. They represent the monetization of thought. As artificial intelligence becomes part of the economy, owning a piece of these systems means holding a share of the world's digital cognition. The potential scale is enormous. Every company, government, and robot that uses computation or AI models will need access to decentralized networks that are faster, cheaper, and more transparent than traditional cloud services.

For the investor, this moment feels similar to the dawn of the internet. The networks are early, the infrastructure is rough, but the direction is clear. The next generation of value will not come from producing raw data. It will come from teaching machines how to understand and use it. That means compute tokens and AI networks could become as essential to the future as oil and electricity once were.

The relationship between blockchain and AI is deeper than convenience. Blockchain provides the trust layer that artificial intelligence has always lacked. A model can make predictions, but without a transparent record of its training and results, no one can verify its honesty. When AI lives on-chain, every model's history can be traced, every data source can be verified, and every reward can be distributed without bias. This transparency builds confidence for investors and users alike.

In practice, decentralized AI means that training a model, hosting a dataset, or sharing GPU power can all become forms of income. A developer in Kenya can earn the same as a developer in New York by contributing compute to Bittensor. A designer in Brazil can rent unused hardware to Render and receive payment directly in tokens. This borderless system is what makes AI on the blockchain such a powerful equalizer. It spreads the wealth of intelligence across the planet.

To gain exposure, investors can look at both tokens and equities. The tokens represent direct participation in decentralized intelligence. The stocks of companies like NVIDIA, AMD, and other chip makers provide exposure to the physical infrastructure that powers these systems. A balanced understanding of both worlds allows an investor to see how hardware and software feed each other. Chips create compute, compute trains models, and models generate value. Each link in the chain offers opportunity.

The future of finance will include portfolios that hold both traditional assets and intelligent networks. AI agents will not just analyze markets; they will take part in them. Imagine a digital assistant that holds a wallet, trades small amounts of crypto to pay for research, and learns which strategies perform best over time. These autonomous investors will eventually exist on the same blockchains we use today. Some may even manage entire funds without human intervention.

This coming economy will blur the line between user and participant. Every person who holds an AI token will help teach, train, or power some part of a global mind. Value will flow to those who supply what the machine economy needs most: computation, creativity, and connectivity.

Decentralized AI is the natural next chapter in the story of technology. It takes the freedom of blockchain and combines it with the intelligence of modern computing. It transforms algorithms into citizens of the digital world. For investors, this is the intelligence dividend. It is the moment when thought itself becomes a resource, measurable, exchangeable, and profitable.

The opportunity is not only financial. It is philosophical. We are witnessing the creation of a marketplace for ideas, where every piece of code can learn, earn, and evolve. The investors who understand this early will not only profit but help shape how intelligence and value grow together.

13

The Tokenization of Everything: Real-World Assets and AI Finance

The digital world is beginning to pull the physical world onto its chain of truth. Every building, bond, artwork, and credit can be represented as a digital token. This process is called tokenization, and it is transforming how people own, trade, and measure value. What once needed banks, brokers, and long contracts can now move through a few lines of verified code. It is the quiet revolution that will bring trillions of dollars from traditional markets into the crypto economy.

At first tokenization sounded like another buzzword. But when you look closer, it becomes clear that this is not about hype. It is about access. The world's wealth has always been locked inside complex systems that only institutions could reach. Tokenization changes that. It lets people own a fraction of anything; real estate, corporate debt, fine art, or a renewable-energy project, and trade it instantly across borders. For the investor, it means liquidity in markets that were once frozen.

Artificial intelligence is playing a key role in this new system. It helps price tokenized assets in real time, scanning global data, market sentiment, and risk signals faster than any human team could. Machine learning models can evaluate real-world assets, adjust collateral levels, and balance digital portfolios with precision. This combination of AI and blockchain forms what many analysts now call AI Finance, a self-learning layer of global liquidity.

Protocols like Chainlink are building the bridges that connect data from the physical world to smart contracts. Its Cross-Chain Interoperability Protocol, or CCIP, allows tokens representing stocks or bonds to move securely across multiple blockchains. Centrifuge uses tokenization to let small businesses finance invoices and earn yield from global lenders. Ondo Finance creates tokenized versions of Treasury bonds and money-market funds so that investors can earn regulated yield inside crypto networks. Even traditional giants like BlackRock are now experimenting with tokenized funds that live both on Wall Street and on-chain.

This shift matters because it changes what it means to invest. In the past, investors chose between traditional and digital assets. In the tokenized future, those categories will merge. A portfolio may hold shares of an energy company, a digital artwork, a property token from Singapore, and a fraction of a solar farm in Kenya; all tracked and settled on the blockchain. Artificial intelligence will handle the complexity, running constant analysis on price movements, yield, and global liquidity.

The opportunity is massive. Analysts estimate that the tokenization of real-world assets could exceed ten trillion dollars in value within the next decade. For investors, that means learning to look for projects that connect these two worlds. The most valuable tokens will not be purely speculative coins but assets backed by something tangible that produces cash flow.

DeFi, or decentralized finance, is evolving into its next stage as a result. What some call DeFi 3.0 blends machine learning, automated lending, and real-world collateral. Imagine an AI agent that continuously scans interest rates, supplies liquidity to the best pools, and exits before market risk grows. These systems are already emerging on decentralized platforms where smart contracts act as autonomous managers. The same intelligence that powers trading algorithms on Wall Street is now open to anyone with a digital wallet.

This creates both freedom and responsibility. Tokenization brings transparency because every transaction is visible, but it also demands care. Smart contracts are code, and code must be audited and maintained. Regulation will soon formalize how tokenized securities can be issued and who can trade them. As the laws mature, the market will stabilize, and early investors who understand the structure will have an advantage.

For those looking to gain exposure, it starts with understanding where tokenization meets AI. Holding tokens from platforms like Chainlink, Centrifuge, or Ondo is one way to participate directly in the infrastructure. Investing in companies that lead in digital-asset custody or compliance gives indirect exposure to the growth of this sector. The key is not chasing yield but following utility. Tokens that solve real problems—access, transparency, or efficiency—will hold their value when speculation fades.

AI finance is changing the rhythm of capital itself. Markets that once closed at night now run continuously. Portfolios update every second. Credit lines appear and dissolve with the movement of data. The investor of the future will rely on machine intelligence as a silent partner. It will analyze trends, hedge risk, and even communicate with other AIs to trade assets at the speed of light.

This is not science fiction; it is already forming. The first tokenized bonds, properties, and carbon credits exist today. They are the foundation of a world where everything valuable can be represented as data and traded globally. Blockchain provides the trust. Artificial intelligence provides the judgment. Together they form the next stage of finance—open, efficient, and inclusive.

The lesson for investors is simple. The most powerful trend in finance is not speculation but transformation. When value becomes liquid, and intelligence becomes automated, the playing field changes forever. Those who understand tokenization now will hold a strategic advantage when traditional finance finally catches up. The tokenization of everything is not coming someday. It is already here, quietly rewriting the balance sheets of the world.

14

Privacy, Zero Knowledge, and Digital Identity in the Machine Age

Every great technology age eventually reaches the same question. Who owns the data? As artificial intelligence and blockchain merge, that question becomes the center of everything. The more connected the world becomes, the more valuable privacy becomes. Information is currency, and whoever controls it holds power. The next stage of crypto will not just be about coins or networks. It will be about protecting the human fingerprint inside the machine economy.

Blockchain gave the world transparency. Every transaction can be traced, verified, and recorded forever. That is what makes it powerful. But transparency without privacy can also expose people. As artificial intelligence begins to process everything on-chain, privacy must evolve. We need systems that can prove truth without revealing every detail. This is where zero-knowledge technology comes in.

A zero-knowledge proof is a cryptographic way to show that something is true without showing how you know it. It lets you prove that a statement is correct without exposing the data behind it. In simple terms, it is like showing a receipt without revealing your entire bank account. These proofs are becoming the backbone of privacy in crypto and artificial intelligence. They allow AI systems to verify identity, training data, or computations without leaking sensitive information.

Projects such as StarkWare, zkSync, and Mina are developing scalable ways to use zero-knowledge proofs in everyday transactions. Developers are now experimenting with ZKML, or zero-knowledge machine learning, which allows an AI to make a decision and prove it followed the correct process without revealing the raw data or model. This technology could protect users from AI bias and secure data ownership in an automated economy.

For investors, zero-knowledge infrastructure represents one of the strongest long-term bets in blockchain technology. It combines compliance with privacy, which is a rare balance. Governments and corporations want systems that are both auditable and secure. ZK-based platforms make that possible. As regulators demand transparency, and users demand privacy, this middle ground becomes essential.

Privacy is not just technical; it is ethical. In a world where AI systems can analyze faces, voices, and purchase histories, the line between data and identity becomes thin. People need a way to control how their identity is used. That is why decentralized identity, or DID, is gaining momentum. A decentralized identity lets users prove who they are without handing control to a corporation. It connects your personal credentials to your own digital wallet instead of a company server.

Projects like Worldcoin, Polygon ID, and Microsoft's ION are exploring this field. Worldcoin uses biometric verification to give every person a unique identity that cannot be duplicated by AI. Polygon ID focuses on self-sovereign identity, where you own your digital passport. Microsoft's ION is building decentralized identifiers that connect to the wider web. Together these efforts form the early framework of digital reputation in the AI economy.

For investors, identity tokens and privacy coins represent a new category of exposure. They are not speculative side projects but infrastructure for a fair digital world. As more people work, trade, and create online, reputation will hold measurable value. A verified digital identity could become as important as a credit score or driver's license. Companies that provide the tools to verify and protect identity will become essential service providers in this new economy.

The same technologies that protect identity will also reshape entertainment and gaming. In the next version of the internet, avatars, property, and personality can live on-chain. This means that your character in a game, your art, and your digital assets are tied to your verified identity. GameFi projects and metaverse worlds will depend on this link to prevent fraud and secure ownership. Artificial intelligence will populate these worlds with intelligent non-player characters that trade, learn, and respond to human behavior. Tokens will flow through them, creating living economies powered by both humans and machines.

The link between privacy, identity, and the metaverse might sound abstract, but it points to a clear investment theme. The next phase of value creation will reward technologies that balance openness with protection. Networks that handle data responsibly will attract long-term adoption from both users and institutions. Privacy is becoming a feature, not a barrier. It is the quiet strength behind the next bull market.

For the modern investor, understanding privacy technology is more than a technical skill. It is a way to future-proof your strategy. As artificial intelligence automates analysis and decision-making, owning assets that safeguard human choice and consent will become vital. It is not about hiding from the system. It is about designing systems that respect individual control.

Zero knowledge, decentralized identity, and AI ethics all converge on one principle: trust through verification. The blockchain world began with the idea of trustless systems. But as machines take over more tasks, we will need a new kind of trust. We will need systems that respect the boundaries between transparency and privacy.

The companies and tokens that solve this challenge will lead the next wave of innovation. They will be the gatekeepers of digital dignity. In the machine age, privacy is no longer about secrecy. It is about ownership. When you control your identity and your data, you are not just a user of technology. You are a shareholder in the future.

15

The Policy Horizon: Regulation and Ethical AI Finance

The world of digital finance is growing fast, but every new system needs rules. The next phase of cryptocurrency and technology will be defined by regulation and ethics. These two ideas may sound distant from innovation, but they shape how money moves and where opportunity grows. The stronger and clearer the rules become, the more confidence investors will have to participate.

Regulation is not a threat to innovation. It is the foundation that allows real growth. The internet did not become a trusted place for commerce until laws protected consumers and businesses. The same will happen for crypto and digital finance. When the rules are in place, larger companies and institutions will enter the market. That is when real adoption begins.

Around the world, new policies are being written. The European Union created MiCA, a framework that defines how crypto projects can operate safely across Europe. The United States continues to clarify how tokens should be classified and traded. Singapore and Japan are developing clear systems that welcome innovation while protecting investors. These efforts signal one thing: the digital economy is becoming part of the global economy.

One major development is the rise of central bank digital currencies, also known as CBDCs. These are digital forms of national currencies that are controlled by governments and run on secure networks. China already uses its digital yuan in daily transactions. The European Union is testing the digital euro. The United States is researching a digital dollar. These systems make it possible to send and receive national currencies quickly and safely, without relying on private companies.

As the world transitions to this new financial era, ethics will matter as much as speed. When machines handle transactions and data, people need to know that their information is secure and used fairly. Transparency, fairness, and data protection will become key parts of every serious digital project. Investors should look for companies and tokens that care about compliance and privacy. The next wave of successful projects will not hide from regulation. They will embrace it.

This is already visible in how major exchanges and projects are preparing for stricter oversight. They publish audits, verify smart contracts, and disclose how they manage funds. They are showing that being open builds trust. Regulation gives investors a way to separate reliable projects from risky ones. It is how the market matures.

Ethical investing is also growing inside this space. People want to know that the technology they support benefits society. Projects that promote financial inclusion, green computing, or responsible data use are starting to attract both private and institutional investors. For anyone building or holding digital assets, ethical practice is now a competitive advantage.

The best way to prepare for this future is to stay informed. Read about new laws, policy updates, and official statements. Watch which countries encourage responsible innovation. Regulation shows where governments plan to focus resources and attention. That knowledge can guide investment decisions long before the market reacts.

The lesson is simple. Regulation creates confidence. Confidence attracts capital. Capital drives innovation. The investors who understand this cycle will be ready when the next stage of digital finance unfolds.

As we move toward a fully connected financial system, the smartest investors will combine innovation with compliance. They will look for clarity, not chaos. When a government sets new standards, it is not closing the door on innovation. It is opening it to a wider audience.

The policy horizon marks a turning point. This is where technology meets accountability and where responsible growth begins. The projects that respect the rules and the people who follow them will become the leaders of the next economy. The market is not being restricted. It is being prepared for scale.

For investors, this is the time to pay attention to structure, ethics, and long-term value. The world is getting ready for a more stable digital economy. The ones who see that now will be ready to thrive when it arrives.

16

The Coinbase Blueprint: How to Future-Proof Your Digital Portfolio

Every investor needs a starting point, and for most people in the United States that starting point is Coinbase. It is one of the most regulated and widely used digital-asset platforms in the world. It provides a simple way to buy, sell, and hold cryptocurrencies while staying inside established financial law. Coinbase is not just a trading app anymore; it has become a bridge between traditional finance and the new digital economy.

This chapter is about how to use Coinbase as the foundation for a strong, secure, and future-ready portfolio. It is not about guessing prices or chasing trends. It is about structure, discipline, and knowledge. With the right approach, Coinbase can give any investor direct exposure to the same technologies that are shaping the next financial era.

Building the Foundation

Coinbase lists hundreds of tokens, but not all of them belong in a serious portfolio. The goal is to recognize which assets represent the pillars of infrastructure, intelligence, and culture. Bitcoin and Ethereum remain the anchors of digital value and long-term trust. Solana and Polygon offer exposure to speed and scale—the qualities that power DePIN systems and advanced applications. Cardano and Algorand emphasize sustainability and strong governance. Together these blockchains form the base of the emerging machine economy.

Beyond these foundational assets, Coinbase now lists a growing set of tokens that represent intelligence and data utility. Render provides decentralized graphics processing power for creators. Fetch AI supports autonomous agents that perform smart transactions. SingularityNET allows developers to share and trade intelligent services. The Graph organizes blockchain data so that machines can find and use information more efficiently. These projects show how intelligence and infrastructure are beginning to merge. For investors, they are early indicators of where digital value is moving.

Coinbase also reflects the cultural side of crypto. Dogecoin and Shiba Inu started as jokes but became global communities that influence markets. They are volatile, yet they demonstrate how culture and humor can translate into economic energy. Small, measured exposure to cultural tokens can help investors understand how attention itself has become a form of value.

Using Coinbase the Right Way

The most effective way to use Coinbase is to think long term. Build a foundation of quality assets and add new exposure slowly. Avoid short-term speculation. Focus on coins and companies with real teams, transparent goals, and measurable impact. Coinbase's listing standards already filter out much of the noise, but personal discipline is what protects results.

Security should come first. Enable two-factor authentication, keep backup copies of recovery phrases, and use hardware wallets for significant holdings. Maintain clean records for tax reporting and staking income. Treat the account as part of your professional financial plan, not a social experiment.

Coinbase continues to evolve beyond a simple exchange. Its own blockchain, called Base, is designed for faster and cheaper transactions. Developers are building next-generation apps on it that connect to AI, DePIN, and digital-identity projects. Understanding Base early gives investors an edge because it shows how Coinbase intends to remain a permanent part of the intelligent economy rather than just a gateway.

Staking is another feature worth attention. When you stake tokens such as Ethereum or Solana, you help secure the network and earn yield in return. This creates passive exposure to blockchain activity without the need for constant trading. It is a slow and steady method of growth that matches the rhythm of real investing.

A future-ready investor uses Coinbase not only to buy coins but to learn. The platform offers research tools, price tracking, and educational resources. Study how AI tokens, DePIN networks, and core blockchains interact. Over time, patterns appear, and those patterns become strategies. Knowledge converts randomness into purpose.

Coinbase itself is not a promise of profit. It is a safe classroom and a long-term platform. The investors who use it with patience and curiosity will benefit most as digital adoption expands. Each token inside your account represents a small piece of tomorrow's financial system: Bitcoin and Ethereum for trust, Solana and Polygon for scale, Render and Fetch AI for intelligence, Helium and Filecoin for physical connectivity. Together they tell the story of where the world is going.

Millions of new participants will enter this market in the next decade. Many will start right here. The difference between those who succeed and those who fail will be knowledge and self-control. Investing is not gambling. It is participation in building the next economy.

Final Takeaway Stack: The Coinbase Blueprint

Coinbase is the bridge between traditional finance and the digital future. It gives investors a regulated, transparent entry into blockchain, intelligence, and innovation.

A durable portfolio begins with proven assets such as Bitcoin and Ethereum. Solana, Polygon, Cardano, and Algorand add speed, scale, and sustainability, forming the technological base of the new economy.

Tokens like Render, Fetch AI, SingularityNET, and The Graph bring exposure to the intelligence layer where computation and automation create real productivity. DePIN projects such as Helium, Filecoin, and Akash connect digital networks to the physical world and form the infrastructure of machine-to-machine commerce.

Cultural tokens including Dogecoin and Shiba Inu remind investors that emotion and creativity influence markets as much as data and code.

Security remains the heart of every portfolio. Protect your account, maintain backups, and apply the same professionalism you would to any other investment.

Staking and earning programs are not side features; they are ways to take part in network growth and receive yield aligned with the system's success.

Base, the blockchain built by Coinbase, signals the company's long-term vision. It will support faster transactions and host new applications that blend finance, identity, and data. Learning how it works today prepares you for the technologies of tomorrow.

Education is the greatest edge. Use Coinbase's tools to understand the purpose behind every token. Follow the interaction between AI projects, DePIN systems, and major blockchains. Insight is what turns speculation into intelligent investing.

Coinbase is more than an exchange. It is a living financial hub that evolves with the economy. When used with patience, integrity, and attention, it becomes a reliable partner in wealth building.

The path forward is clear. Build gradually. Hold assets that represent progress. Stay transparent, secure, and informed. Investors who follow these principles will not just adapt to the future. They will help define it.

17

The Machine Economy Is Here

The world is changing faster than most people realize. Every day, machines are learning to think, trade, and act on their own. The signals are already around us. A car drives itself through city streets and sells its driving data to a network. A home battery trades power with the grid while the owner sleeps. A warehouse of robots orders spare parts before anything breaks. Behind each of those actions is code that records, verifies, and pays. Machines are learning to earn, and they are already part of the economy that we once believed belonged only to us.

We have reached a point where technology is not just helping us work but becoming part of how value moves. Artificial intelligence gives systems the ability to learn and improve. Blockchain gives them memory and accountability. Quantum computing gives them speed and precision beyond anything we have seen before. Together they form a living infrastructure that connects thought, action, and trust. The machine economy is not a dream. It exists today.

When I began writing about artificial intelligence and blockchain, I wanted to understand how these technologies would collide. What I discovered is that they were never meant to be separate. Intelligence needs trust, and trust needs memory. That memory lives on the blockchain. Machines cannot cooperate unless they know what others have done. Blockchain gives them a shared history that keeps them honest. That is how intelligence becomes economic.

Value once moved through human hands. Now it moves through intelligent systems. The first industrial revolution gave us machines that worked. The digital revolution gave us machines that communicated. This new revolution gives us machines that decide. They do not replace us; they expand what we can build. We are creating an economy of systems that think, connect, and create.

The investors of this new world will not just look for products or services. They will look for networks of intelligence. They will ask where the data flows, where the compute lives, and where the trust is recorded. The map of opportunity stretches across chips, nodes, and algorithms. Hardware companies such as NVIDIA, AMD, TSMC, and Broadcom supply the muscle. Projects such as Helium, Render, and Akash reward people for sharing bandwidth, storage, and computing power. Platforms like Bittensor, Fetch AI, Ocean Protocol, and SingularityNET let algorithms exchange data and learning. Core blockchains such as Bitcoin, Ethereum, Solana, and Algorand hold the base layer of truth. Quantum pioneers such as IBM, Google, and IonQ prepare the next level of speed and computation that will link everything together. Each layer supports the others. Hardware powers intelligence. Intelligence drives blockchains. Blockchains secure the world's collective data.

Understanding these layers is the foundation of smart investing. Hardware generates energy for thought. Software organizes that thought. Artificial intelligence interprets the data. Blockchain keeps the record true. The result is an economy that never sleeps. Machines work in real time, moving value in microscopic transactions that together sustain entire industries. You might not see it, but it happens constantly.

The modern investor watches how intelligence spreads and studies where automation meets trust. The focus is not on the noise of the moment but on the flow of innovation. The strongest opportunities come from networks that have clear users, useful technology, and open design. Volatility is no longer a verdict. It is a measure of adoption in progress. The best strategy is not to chase the next coin but to understand how this new system breathes. The machine economy is not about trading symbols; it is about reading signals.

Artificial intelligence has already proven that knowledge can scale. A single model can serve millions of people at once. Blockchain proves that trust can exist without intermediaries. Quantum computing will show that processing power can move beyond current limits. Combined, these technologies create a civilization that runs on verified intelligence. It is a web of connection that transforms data into decision and decision into value.

Even in this new world, human imagination remains the true source of everything. Machines can calculate, but they cannot hope or dream. They can reason, but they cannot choose purpose. They are extensions of our creativity. The real promise of the machine economy is not automation; it is amplification. When we use technology with discipline and vision, we turn power into possibility.

This new era is not only about wealth. It is about connection and balance. Machines will distribute resources where they are needed, manage energy grids, monitor health, and protect digital infrastructure. They will not replace people. They will serve us by handling what we cannot do alone. The real question is how we will guide them.

In the future, every device can become its own business. Every system can act as an entrepreneur. Every network can function as a marketplace. And every person who understands this transformation can help shape it. We are moving into a world that trades not only currency but intelligence.

If you take anything from this book, let it be this: the machine economy is already here. It is growing beneath our cities, our screens, and our daily routines. The question is not whether it will happen, but how we will participate. The builders, investors, and thinkers who recognize this shift early will not only profit from it; they will define it.

This is the moment to act with awareness, to invest with purpose, and to create with integrity. The future is not waiting for permission. It has already begun, and it belongs to those who see intelligence as progress, not competition.

The machines are learning to earn. Our responsibility is to make sure they earn for everyone.

GLOSSARY OF KEY TERMS

Address:

A unique string of letters and numbers that represents a digital wallet on a blockchain. It is where coins are sent or received.

AI (Artificial Intelligence):

Computer systems that learn, reason, or make decisions like humans. AI powers chatbots, robots, and smart algorithms.

Algorithm:

A set of rules that tells a computer how to solve a problem or make a decision.

Altcoin:

Any cryptocurrency that is not Bitcoin. Examples include Ethereum, Solana, and Shiba Inu.

API (Application Programming Interface):

A bridge that lets one computer program talk to another and share data or services.

Blockchain:

A digital ledger that records transactions across many computers so that the data cannot be changed or erased.

Block:

A group of verified transactions added to a blockchain. Each block connects to the one before it.

Consensus Mechanism:

The process that blockchains use to agree on which transactions are valid. Examples are Proof of Work and Proof of Stake.

Cryptocurrency (Crypto):

Digital money that uses encryption to control its creation and verify transfers without banks.

DAO (Decentralized Autonomous Organization):

An online community that uses smart contracts and tokens to make collective decisions.

Data Oracle:

A service, like Chainlink, that brings real-world data (weather, prices, sports scores) into a blockchain so smart contracts can react to it.

DeFi (Decentralized Finance):

Financial tools and services that run on blockchain instead of banks—like lending, saving, or trading.

DePIN (Decentralized Physical Infrastructure Network):

A system where people or machines share real-world resources (internet, storage, energy) and earn crypto in return.

DApp (Decentralized Application):

An app that runs on a blockchain using smart contracts instead of a central server.

Encryption:

A way of hiding information using math so only authorized users can read it.

Ethereum:

A major blockchain known for creating smart contracts and decentralized apps.

Fiat Currency:

Government-issued money like the U.S. dollar or euro.

Gas Fee:

The small fee users pay to run transactions or smart contracts on a blockchain.

GPU (Graphics Processing Unit):

A powerful chip used for gaming, AI training, and crypto mining.

Halving:

A programmed event that cuts Bitcoin mining rewards in half every four years to control supply.

Hash:

A short digital fingerprint of data. It proves that information has not been changed.

Hot Wallet / Cold Wallet:

Hot wallets connect to the internet for quick access. Cold wallets stay offline for security.

Layer 1 / Layer 2:

Layer 1 is the main blockchain (like Ethereum). Layer 2 builds on top to make it faster or cheaper (like Arbitrum or Optimism).

Liquidity:

How easily a token can be bought or sold without affecting its price.

Market Capitalization (Market Cap):
The total value of a cryptocurrency. Calculated by multiplying the token price by the number of coins in circulation.

Meme Coin:
A cryptocurrency inspired by internet jokes or culture. Examples are Dogecoin, Shiba Inu, and Pepe Coin.

Mining / Staking:
Mining uses computers to solve puzzles and add blocks. Staking locks coins to help run the network and earn rewards.

NFT (Non-Fungible Token):
A unique digital asset stored on a blockchain, often used for art, collectibles, or game items.

Node:
A computer that keeps a copy of the blockchain and helps verify transactions.

Private Key / Public Key:
A private key lets you spend your crypto—never share it. A public key is your wallet address for receiving funds.

Quantum Computing:
A new kind of computing that uses qubits instead of bits, allowing far greater processing power and potential to break traditional encryption.

Smart Contract:
Self-running code on a blockchain that carries out an agreement automatically when set conditions are met.

Stablecoin:

A crypto token whose value is tied to a stable asset, like the U.S. dollar, to reduce volatility.

Tokenomics:

The economic design of a cryptocurrency—how tokens are created, distributed, and used.

Utility Token:

A coin that gives holders access to a product, service, or reward inside a project's ecosystem.

Wallet:

A digital tool or app that stores your private keys and manages your crypto funds.

Web3:

The next generation of the internet, built on decentralized technologies where users own their data and digital identity.

Whitepaper:

A document that explains how a blockchain project works and why it exists.

Yield Farming:

Earning rewards by lending or staking crypto in DeFi platforms.

WORKS CITED

Akash Network. (2025). Decentralized Cloud Infrastructure Overview.

Algorand Foundation. (2025). *Quantum-Safe Blockchain Research.*

Aptos Foundation. (2024). *Aptos Whitepaper: Move Language Overview.*

Arweave Foundation. (2024). *Permanent Storage Economy Whitepaper.*

Ava Labs. (2024). *Avalanche Subnet Architecture Report.*

Bittensor Foundation. (2025). *Decentralized Intelligence Protocol Whitepaper.*

Broadcom Inc. (2024). *Corporate Semiconductor Innovation Overview.*

Buterin, V. (2015). *Ethereum Whitepaper: A Next-Generation Smart Contract Platform.*

Cardano Foundation. (2025).

Lattice-Based Cryptography Studies and Blockchain Governance Paper.

Celestia Labs. (2024). *Modular Blockchain Design Overview.*

Chainlink (SmartContract Ltd.). (2024). *Chainlink Decentralized Oracle Network Whitepaper.*

CoinDesk Research. (2025). *Top Blockchain Networks and Ecosystem Analysis.*

DFINITY Foundation. (2024). *Internet Computer Developer Report.*

Dogecoin Foundation. (2024). *Dogecoin Community and Development Overview.*

D-Wave Systems. (2025). *Quantum Annealing for Optimization.*

Energy Web Foundation. (2024). *Decentralized Energy Infrastructure Report.*

Ethereum Foundation. (2025). *Smart Contract Development Overview.*

Fetch.ai. (2025). *Autonomous Economic Agents Research.*

Flow Foundation. (2024). *Blockchain for Digital Creation Report.*

Google AI Quantum Team. (2019).

Quantum Supremacy Using a Programmable

Superconducting Processor. Nature, 574(7779), 505–510.

Helium Foundation. (2024). *The People's Network: Global Coverage Expansion.*

Hedera Council. (2024). *Hashgraph Consensus Technical Paper.*

Hivemapper. (2024). *Decentralized Mapping Protocol Whitepaper.*

Hoskinson, C. (2020). *Cardano Design Philosophy.* Cardano Foundation Research Notes.

IBM Research. (2025). *IBM Quantum Network Developer Program.*

IonQ. (2025). *Trapped-Ion Quantum Computing Overview.*

IoTeX Foundation. (2025). *Trusted Machine Economy Report.*

Kaspa Community. (2025). *Parallel Proof-of-Work Whitepaper.*

Kwon, J. (2019). *Cosmos: The Internet of Blockchains.* Interchain Foundation.

McKinsey & Company. (2024). *The State of AI and Robotics in Industry.*

National Institute of Standards and Technology (NIST). (2025).

Post-Quantum Cryptography Standards and Guidance.

Near Foundation. (2024). *NEAR Developer Overview.*

Nakamoto, S. (2008). *Bitcoin: A Peer-to-Peer Electronic Cash System.* Bitcoin Foundation.

Offchain Labs. (2024). *Arbitrum Rollup Whitepaper.*

Optimism Foundation. (2024). *Public Goods Funding and Layer 2 Governance Report.*

Ocean Protocol Foundation. (2024). *Data Marketplace Framework.*

Palantir Technologies Inc. (2024). *AI-Driven Data Analytics Platform Overview.*

Polkadot Foundation. (2024). *Parachain Connection Model and Relay Chain Design.*

Protocol Labs. (2024). *Filecoin Network Report: Decentralized Storage Economy.*

Render Network Foundation. (2025). *Distributed GPU Economy for AI and Digital Media.*

Rigetti Computing. (2025). *Hybrid Quantum-Classical Systems Whitepaper.*

Ripple Labs. (2024). *Cross-Border Payment System Overview.*

Shiba Inu Ecosystem. (2025). *Shibarium Layer 2 Network Documentation.*

SingularityNET Foundation. (2024). *AI Marketplace and Decentralized Governance*

Overview.

Solana Foundation. (2025). *Solana Developer and DePIN Infrastructure Report.*

Stellar Development Foundation. (2024). *Cross-Border Remittance and Financial Inclusion*

Study.

Sui Foundation. (2025). *Sui Architecture Overview.*

Tezos Foundation. (2024). *Self-Amending Blockchain Governance Report.*

TON Foundation. (2025). *The Open Network Overview.*

Tron Foundation. (2024). *Decentralized Content Economy Whitepaper.*

VeChain Foundation. (2024). *Supply Chain Transparency Report.*

WeatherXM. (2025). *Community-Powered Weather Networks Report.*

Wood, G. (2020). *Polkadot: The Multi-Chain Framework.* Parity Technologies.

Yakovenko, A. (2020). *Solana: Proof of History Design Paper.* Solana Labs.

www.ingramcontent.com/pod-product-compliance
Lightning Source LLC
La Vergne TN
LVHW040516210926
848480LV00005BA/1478
9798349642890